Internet Password Organizer™

The Practical Solution To Password Pollution™

Internet Password Organizer™

If found please contact:

Name: _____

Phone: _____

Email: _____

Warning and Disclaimer

Every effort has been made to make this book as complete and accurate as possible, but no warranty or fitness is implied. The information provided is on an "as is" basis. The author and the publisher shall have neither liability nor responsibility to any person or entity with respect to any loss or damages arising from the information contained, or subsequently stored, in this book.

Web Page:

Username:

Password:

Notes:

Web Page:

Username:

Password:

Notes:

Web Page:

Username:

Password:

Notes:

Web Page:

Username:

Password:

Notes:

Web Page:

Username:

Password:

Notes:

Web Page:

Username:

Password:

Notes:

Web Page:

Username:

Password:

Notes:

Web Page:

Username:

Password:

Notes:

Web Page:

Username:

Password:

Notes:

Web Page:

Username:

Password:

Notes:

A

Web Page:

Username:

Password:

Notes:

Web Page:

Username:

Password:

Notes:

Web Page:

Username:

Password:

Notes:

Web Page:

Username:

Password:

Notes:

Web Page:

Username:

Password:

Notes:

A

Web Page: _____

Username: _____

Password: _____

Notes: _____

_____

_____

Web Page: _____

Username: _____

Password: _____

Notes: _____

_____

_____

Web Page: _____

Username: _____

Password: _____

Notes: _____

_____

_____

Web Page: _____

Username: _____

Password: _____

Notes: _____

_____

_____

Web Page: _____

Username: _____

Password: _____

Notes: _____

_____

_____

Web Page:

Username:

Password:

Notes:

Web Page:

Username:

Password:

Notes:

Web Page:

Username:

Password:

Notes:

Web Page:

Username:

Password:

Notes:

Web Page:

Username:

Password:

Notes:

B

Web Page:

Username:

Password:

Notes:

Web Page:

Username:

Password:

Notes:

Web Page:

Username:

Password:

Notes:

Web Page:

Username:

Password:

Notes:

Web Page:

Username:

Password:

Notes:

Web Page:

Username:

Password:

Notes:

Web Page:

Username:

Password:

Notes:

Web Page:

Username:

Password:

Notes:

Web Page:

Username:

Password:

Notes:

Web Page:

Username:

Password:

Notes:

B

Web Page:

Username:

Password:

Notes:

Web Page:

Username:

Password:

Notes:

Web Page:

Username:

Password:

Notes:

Web Page:

Username:

Password:

Notes:

Web Page:

Username:

Password:

Notes:

Web Page:

Username:

Password:

Notes:

Web Page:

Username:

Password:

Notes:

Web Page:

Username:

Password:

Notes:

Web Page:

Username:

Password:

Notes:

Web Page:

Username:

Password:

Notes:

C

Web Page:

Username:

Password:

Notes:

Web Page:

Username:

Password:

Notes:

Web Page:

Username:

Password:

Notes:

Web Page:

Username:

Password:

Notes:

Web Page:

Username:

Password:

Notes:

Web Page:

Username:

Password:

Notes:

Web Page:

Username:

Password:

Notes:

Web Page:

Username:

Password:

Notes:

Web Page:

Username:

Password:

Notes:

Web Page:

Username:

Password:

Notes:

C

Web Page: _____

Username: _____

Password: _____

Notes: _____

_____

Web Page: _____

Username: _____

Password: _____

Notes: _____

_____

Web Page: _____

Username: _____

Password: _____

Notes: _____

_____

Web Page: _____

Username: _____

Password: _____

Notes: _____

_____

Web Page: _____

Username: _____

Password: _____

Notes: _____

_____

Web Page:

Username:

Password:

Notes:

Web Page:

Username:

Password:

Notes:

Web Page:

Username:

Password:

Notes:

Web Page:

Username:

Password:

Notes:

Web Page:

Username:

Password:

Notes:

D

Web Page: _____

Username: _____

Password: _____

Notes: _____

_____

_____

Web Page: _____

Username: _____

Password: _____

Notes: _____

_____

_____

Web Page: _____

Username: _____

Password: _____

Notes: _____

_____

_____

Web Page: _____

Username: _____

Password: _____

Notes: _____

_____

_____

Web Page: _____

Username: _____

Password: _____

Notes: _____

_____

_____

Web Page:

Username:

Password:

Notes:

Web Page:

Username:

Password:

Notes:

Web Page:

Username:

Password:

Notes:

Web Page:

Username:

Password:

Notes:

Web Page:

Username:

Password:

Notes:

D

Web Page:

Username:

Password:

Notes:

Web Page:

Username:

Password:

Notes:

Web Page:

Username:

Password:

Notes:

Web Page:

Username:

Password:

Notes:

Web Page:

Username:

Password:

Notes:

Web Page:

Username:

Password:

Notes:

Web Page:

Username:

Password:

Notes:

Web Page:

Username:

Password:

Notes:

Web Page:

Username:

Password:

Notes:

Web Page:

Username:

Password:

Notes:

E

Web Page: _____

Username: _____

Password: _____

Notes: _____

_____

Web Page: _____

Username: _____

Password: _____

Notes: _____

_____

Web Page: _____

Username: _____

Password: _____

Notes: _____

_____

Web Page: _____

Username: _____

Password: _____

Notes: _____

_____

Web Page: _____

Username: _____

Password: _____

Notes: _____

_____

Web Page:

Username:

Password:

Notes:

Web Page:

Username:

Password:

Notes:

Web Page:

Username:

Password:

Notes:

Web Page:

Username:

Password:

Notes:

Web Page:

Username:

Password:

Notes:

E

Web Page: _____

Username: _____

Password: _____

Notes: _____

_____

Web Page: _____

Username: _____

Password: _____

Notes: _____

_____

Web Page: _____

Username: _____

Password: _____

Notes: _____

_____

Web Page: _____

Username: _____

Password: _____

Notes: _____

_____

Web Page: _____

Username: _____

Password: _____

Notes: _____

_____

Web Page:

Username:

Password:

Notes:

Web Page:

Username:

Password:

Notes:

Web Page:

Username:

Password:

Notes:

Web Page:

Username:

Password:

Notes:

Web Page:

Username:

Password:

Notes:

F

Web Page:

Username:

Password:

Notes:

Web Page:

Username:

Password:

Notes:

Web Page:

Username:

Password:

Notes:

Web Page:

Username:

Password:

Notes:

Web Page:

Username:

Password:

Notes:

Web Page:

Username:

Password:

Notes:

Web Page:

Username:

Password:

Notes:

Web Page:

Username:

Password:

Notes:

Web Page:

Username:

Password:

Notes:

Web Page:

Username:

Password:

Notes:

F

Web Page:

Username:

Password:

Notes:

Web Page:

Username:

Password:

Notes:

Web Page:

Username:

Password:

Notes:

Web Page:

Username:

Password:

Notes:

Web Page:

Username:

Password:

Notes:

Web Page:

Username:

Password:

Notes:

Web Page:

Username:

Password:

Notes:

Web Page:

Username:

Password:

Notes:

Web Page:

Username:

Password:

Notes:

Web Page:

Username:

Password:

Notes:

Web Page: _____

Username: _____

Password: _____

Notes: _____

_____

_____

Web Page: _____

Username: _____

Password: _____

Notes: _____

_____

_____

Web Page: _____

Username: _____

Password: _____

Notes: _____

_____

_____

Web Page: _____

Username: _____

Password: _____

Notes: _____

_____

_____

Web Page: _____

Username: _____

Password: _____

Notes: _____

_____

_____

Web Page:

Username:

Password:

Notes:

Web Page:

Username:

Password:

Notes:

Web Page:

Username:

Password:

Notes:

Web Page:

Username:

Password:

Notes:

Web Page:

Username:

Password:

Notes:

G

Web Page: _____

Username: _____

Password: _____

Notes: _____

_____

Web Page: _____

Username: _____

Password: _____

Notes: _____

_____

Web Page: _____

Username: _____

Password: _____

Notes: _____

_____

Web Page: _____

Username: _____

Password: _____

Notes: _____

_____

Web Page: _____

Username: _____

Password: _____

Notes: _____

_____

Web Page:

Username:

Password:

Notes:

Web Page:

Username:

Password:

Notes:

Web Page:

Username:

Password:

Notes:

Web Page:

Username:

Password:

Notes:

Web Page:

Username:

Password:

Notes:

Web Page: _____

Username: _____

Password: _____

Notes: _____

_____

_____

Web Page: _____

Username: _____

H Password: _____

Notes: _____

_____

_____

Web Page: _____

Username: _____

Password: _____

Notes: _____

_____

_____

Web Page: _____

Username: _____

Password: _____

Notes: _____

_____

_____

Web Page: _____

Username: _____

Password: _____

Notes: _____

_____

_____

Web Page:

Username:

Password:

Notes:

Web Page:

Username:

Password:

Notes:

Web Page:

Username:

Password:

Notes:

Web Page:

Username:

Password:

Notes:

Web Page:

Username:

Password:

Notes:

Web Page:

Username:

Password:

Notes:

Web Page:

Username:

H Password:

Notes:

Web Page:

Username:

Password:

Notes:

Web Page:

Username:

Password:

Notes:

Web Page:

Username:

Password:

Notes:

Web Page:

Username:

Password:

Notes:

Web Page:

Username:

Password:

Notes:

Web Page:

Username:

Password:

Notes:

Web Page:

Username:

Password:

Notes:

Web Page:

Username:

Password:

Notes:

Web Page:

Username:

Password:

Notes:

Web Page:

Username:

Password:

I Notes:

Web Page:

Username:

Password:

Notes:

Web Page:

Username:

Password:

Notes:

Web Page:

Username:

Password:

Notes:

Web Page:

Username:

Password:

Notes:

Web Page:

Username:

Password:

Notes:

I

Web Page:

Username:

Password:

Notes:

Web Page:

Username:

Password:

Notes:

Web Page:

Username:

Password:

Notes:

Web Page: _____

Username: _____

Password: _____

Notes: _____

_____

_____

Web Page: _____

Username: _____

Password: _____

Notes: _____

_____

_____

Web Page: _____

Username: _____

Password: _____

Notes: _____

_____

_____

Web Page: _____

Username: _____

Password: _____

Notes: _____

_____

_____

Web Page: _____

Username: _____

Password: _____

Notes: _____

_____

_____

Web Page:

Username:

Password:

Notes:

Web Page:

Username:

Password:

Notes:

I

Web Page:

Username:

Password:

Notes:

Web Page:

Username:

Password:

Notes:

Web Page:

Username:

Password:

Notes:

Web Page:

Username:

Password:

Notes:

Web Page:

Username:

Password:

Notes:

J

Web Page:

Username:

Password:

Notes:

Web Page:

Username:

Password:

Notes:

Web Page:

Username:

Password:

Notes:

Web Page:

Username:

Password:

Notes:

Web Page:

Username:

Password:

Notes:

Web Page:

Username:

Password:

Notes:

Web Page:

Username:

Password:

Notes:

Web Page:

Username:

Password:

Notes:

Web Page: _____

Username: _____

Password: _____

Notes: _____

_____

Web Page: _____

Username: _____

Password: _____

Notes: _____

J

_____

Web Page: _____

Username: _____

Password: _____

Notes: _____

_____

Web Page: _____

Username: _____

Password: _____

Notes: _____

_____

Web Page: _____

Username: _____

Password: _____

Notes: _____

_____

Web Page:

Username:

Password:

Notes:

Web Page:

Username:

Password:

Notes:

Web Page:

Username:

Password:

Notes:

Web Page:

Username:

Password:

Notes:

Web Page:

Username:

Password:

Notes:

Web Page:

Username:

Password:

Notes:

Web Page:

Username:

Password:

Notes:

K

Web Page:

Username:

Password:

Notes:

Web Page:

Username:

Password:

Notes:

Web Page:

Username:

Password:

Notes:

Web Page:

Username:

Password:

Notes:

Web Page:

Username:

Password:

Notes:

K

Web Page:

Username:

Password:

Notes:

Web Page:

Username:

Password:

Notes:

Web Page:

Username:

Password:

Notes:

Web Page: _____

Username: _____

Password: _____

Notes: _____

_____

Web Page: _____

Username: _____

Password: _____

Notes: _____

_____

K

Web Page: _____

Username: _____

Password: _____

Notes: _____

_____

Web Page: _____

Username: _____

Password: _____

Notes: _____

_____

Web Page: _____

Username: _____

Password: _____

Notes: _____

_____

Web Page:

Username:

Password:

Notes:

Web Page:

Username:

Password:

Notes:

K

Web Page:

Username:

Password:

Notes:

Web Page:

Username:

Password:

Notes:

Web Page:

Username:

Password:

Notes:

Web Page: _____

Username: _____

Password: _____

Notes: _____

_____

Web Page: _____

Username: _____

Password: _____

Notes: _____

_____

L

Web Page: _____

Username: _____

Password: _____

Notes: _____

_____

Web Page: _____

Username: _____

Password: _____

Notes: _____

_____

Web Page: _____

Username: _____

Password: _____

Notes: _____

_____

Web Page:

Username:

Password:

Notes:

Web Page:

Username:

Password:

Notes:

L

Web Page:

Username:

Password:

Notes:

Web Page:

Username:

Password:

Notes:

Web Page:

Username:

Password:

Notes:

Web Page:

Username:

Password:

Notes:

Web Page:

Username:

Password:

Notes:

L

Web Page:

Username:

Password:

Notes:

Web Page:

Username:

Password:

Notes:

Web Page:

Username:

Password:

Notes:

Web Page:

Username:

Password:

Notes:

Web Page:

Username:

Password:

Notes:

Web Page:

L

Username:

Password:

Notes:

Web Page:

Username:

Password:

Notes:

Web Page:

Username:

Password:

Notes:

Web Page:

Username:

Password:

Notes:

Web Page:

Username:

Password:

Notes:

M

Web Page:

Username:

Password:

Notes:

Web Page:

Username:

Password:

Notes:

Web Page:

Username:

Password:

Notes:

Web Page:

Username:

Password:

Notes:

Web Page:

Username:

Password:

Notes:

Web Page:

Username:

Password:

Notes:

M

Web Page:

Username:

Password:

Notes:

Web Page:

Username:

Password:

Notes:

Web Page:

Username:

Password:

Notes:

Web Page:

Username:

Password:

Notes:

M

Web Page:

Username:

Password:

Notes:

Web Page:

Username:

Password:

Notes:

Web Page:

Username:

Password:

Notes:

Web Page:

Username:

Password:

Notes:

Web Page:

Username:

Password:

Notes:

Web Page:

Username:

Password:

Notes:

M

Web Page:

Username:

Password:

Notes:

Web Page:

Username:

Password:

Notes:

Web Page:

Username:

Password:

Notes:

Web Page:

Username:

Password:

Notes:

N

Web Page:

Username:

Password:

Notes:

Web Page:

Username:

Password:

Notes:

Web Page:

Username:

Password:

Notes:

Web Page:

Username:

Password:

Notes:

Web Page:

Username:

Password:

Notes:

Web Page:

Username:

Password:

Notes:

N

Web Page:

Username:

Password:

Notes:

Web Page:

Username:

Password:

Notes:

Web Page: _____

Username: _____

Password: _____

Notes: _____

_____

_____

Web Page: _____

Username: _____

Password: _____

Notes: _____

_____

_____

N Web Page: _____

Username: _____

Password: _____

Notes: _____

_____

_____

Web Page: _____

Username: _____

Password: _____

Notes: _____

_____

_____

Web Page: _____

Username: _____

Password: _____

Notes: _____

_____

_____

Web Page:

Username:

Password:

Notes:

Web Page:

Username:

Password:

Notes:

Web Page:

Username:

Password:

Notes:

N

Web Page:

Username:

Password:

Notes:

Web Page:

Username:

Password:

Notes:

Web Page:

Username:

Password:

Notes:

Web Page:

Username:

Password:

Notes:

Web Page:

Username:

Password:

Notes:

O

Web Page:

Username:

Password:

Notes:

Web Page:

Username:

Password:

Notes:

Web Page:

Username:

Password:

Notes:

Web Page:

Username:

Password:

Notes:

Web Page:

Username:

Password:

Notes:

O

Web Page:

Username:

Password:

Notes:

Web Page:

Username:

Password:

Notes:

Web Page:

Username:

Password:

Notes:

Web Page:

Username:

Password:

Notes:

Web Page:

Username:

Password:

Notes:

O

Web Page:

Username:

Password:

Notes:

Web Page:

Username:

Password:

Notes:

Web Page:

Username:

Password:

Notes:

Web Page:

Username:

Password:

Notes:

Web Page:

Username:

Password:

Notes:

O

Web Page:

Username:

Password:

Notes:

Web Page:

Username:

Password:

Notes:

Web Page:

Username:

Password:

Notes:

Web Page:

Username:

Password:

Notes:

Web Page:

Username:

Password:

Notes:

P

Web Page:

Username:

Password:

Notes:

Web Page:

Username:

Password:

Notes:

Web Page:

Username:

Password:

Notes:

Web Page:

Username:

Password:

Notes:

Web Page:

Username:

Password:

Notes:

Web Page:

Username:

Password:

Notes:

Web Page:

Username:

Password:

Notes:

Web Page:

Username:

Password:

Notes:

Web Page:

Username:

Password:

Notes:

Web Page:

Username:

Password:

Notes:

P

Web Page:

Username:

Password:

Notes:

Web Page:

Username:

Password:

Notes:

Web Page:

Username:

Password:

Notes:

Web Page:

Username:

Password:

Notes:

Web Page:

Username:

Password:

Notes:

P

Web Page:

Username:

Password:

Notes:

Web Page:

Username:

Password:

Notes:

Web Page:

Username:

Password:

Notes:

Web Page:

Username:

Password:

Notes:

Web Page:

Username:

Password:

Notes:

Q Web Page:

Username:

Password:

Notes:

Web Page:

Username:

Password:

Notes:

Web Page:

Username:

Password:

Notes:

Web Page:

Username:

Password:

Notes:

Web Page:

Username:

Password:

Notes:

Web Page:

Username:

Password:

Notes:

Q

Web Page:

Username:

Password:

Notes:

Web Page:

Username:

Password:

Notes:

Web Page:

Username:

Password:

Notes:

Web Page:

Username:

Password:

Notes:

Q

Web Page:

Username:

Password:

Notes:

Web Page:

Username:

Password:

Notes:

Web Page:

Username:

Password:

Notes:

Web Page:

Username:

Password:

Notes:

Web Page:

Username:

Password:

Notes:

Web Page:

Username:

Password:

Notes:

Q

Web Page:

Username:

Password:

Notes:

Web Page: _____

Username: _____

Password: _____

Notes: _____

_____

_____

Web Page: _____

Username: _____

Password: _____

Notes: _____

_____

_____

Web Page: _____

Username: _____

Password: _____

Notes: _____

_____

_____

R

Web Page: _____

Username: _____

Password: _____

Notes: _____

_____

_____

Web Page: _____

Username: _____

Password: _____

Notes: _____

_____

_____

Web Page:

Username:

Password:

Notes:

Web Page:

Username:

Password:

Notes:

Web Page:

Username:

Password:

Notes:

Web Page:

Username:

Password:

Notes:

R

Web Page:

Username:

Password:

Notes:

Web Page:

Username:

Password:

Notes:

Web Page:

Username:

Password:

Notes:

Web Page:

Username:

Password:

Notes:

R

Web Page:

Username:

Password:

Notes:

Web Page:

Username:

Password:

Notes:

Web Page:

Username:

Password:

Notes:

Web Page:

Username:

Password:

Notes:

Web Page:

Username:

Password:

Notes:

Web Page:

Username:

Password:

Notes:

R

Web Page:

Username:

Password:

Notes:

Web Page:

Username:

Password:

Notes:

Web Page:

Username:

Password:

Notes:

Web Page:

Username:

Password:

Notes:

S

Web Page:

Username:

Password:

Notes:

Web Page:

Username:

Password:

Notes:

Web Page:

Username:

Password:

Notes:

Web Page:

Username:

Password:

Notes:

Web Page:

Username:

Password:

Notes:

Web Page:

Username:

Password:

Notes:

S

Web Page:

Username:

Password:

Notes:

Web Page:

Username:

Password:

Notes:

Web Page:

Username:

Password:

Notes:

Web Page:

Username:

Password:

Notes:

S

Web Page:

Username:

Password:

Notes:

Web Page:

Username:

Password:

Notes:

Web Page:

Username:

Password:

Notes:

Web Page:

Username:

Password:

Notes:

Web Page:

Username:

Password:

Notes:

Web Page:

Username:

Password:

Notes:

S

Web Page:

Username:

Password:

Notes:

Web Page:

Username:

Password:

Notes:

Web Page:

Username:

Password:

Notes:

Web Page:

Username:

Password:

Notes:

Web Page:

Username:

Password:

Notes:

T

Web Page:

Username:

Password:

Notes:

Web Page:

Username:

Password:

Notes:

Web Page:

Username:

Password:

Notes:

Web Page:

Username:

Password:

Notes:

Web Page:

Username:

Password:

Notes:

T

Web Page:

Username:

Password:

Notes:

Web Page:

Username:

Password:

Notes:

Web Page:

Username:

Password:

Notes:

Web Page:

Username:

Password:

Notes:

Web Page:

Username:

Password:

Notes:

T

Web Page:

Username:

Password:

Notes:

Web Page:

Username:

Password:

Notes:

Web Page:

Username:

Password:

Notes:

Web Page:

Username:

Password:

Notes:

Web Page:

Username:

Password:

Notes:

T

Web Page:

Username:

Password:

Notes:

Web Page: _____

Username: _____

Password: _____

Notes: _____

_____

_____

Web Page: _____

Username: _____

Password: _____

Notes: _____

_____

_____

Web Page: _____

Username: _____

Password: _____

Notes: _____

_____

_____

Web Page: _____

Username: _____

Password: _____

Notes: _____

_____

U

Web Page: _____

Username: _____

Password: _____

Notes: _____

_____

_____

Web Page:

Username:

Password:

Notes:

Web Page:

Username:

Password:

Notes:

Web Page:

Username:

Password:

Notes:

Web Page:

Username:

Password:

Notes:

U

Web Page:

Username:

Password:

Notes:

Web Page:

Username:

Password:

Notes:

Web Page:

Username:

Password:

Notes:

Web Page:

Username:

Password:

Notes:

Web Page:

Username:

Password:

Notes:

U

Web Page:

Username:

Password:

Notes:

Web Page:

Username:

Password:

Notes:

Web Page:

Username:

Password:

Notes:

Web Page:

Username:

Password:

Notes:

Web Page:

Username:

Password:

Notes:

U

Web Page:

Username:

Password:

Notes:

Web Page:

Username:

Password:

Notes:

Web Page:

Username:

Password:

Notes:

Web Page:

Username:

Password:

Notes:

Web Page:

Username:

Password:

Notes:

V

Web Page:

Username:

Password:

Notes:

Web Page:

Username:

Password:

Notes:

Web Page:

Username:

Password:

Notes:

Web Page:

Username:

Password:

Notes:

Web Page:

Username:

Password:

Notes:

Web Page:

Username:

Password:

Notes:

V

Web Page:

Username:

Password:

Notes:

Web Page:

Username:

Password:

Notes:

Web Page:

Username:

Password:

Notes:

Web Page:

Username:

Password:

Notes:

V

Web Page:

Username:

Password:

Notes:

Web Page:

Username:

Password:

Notes:

Web Page:

Username:

Password:

Notes:

Web Page:

Username:

Password:

Notes:

Web Page:

Username:

Password:

Notes:

Web Page:

Username:

Password:

Notes:

V

Web Page:

Username:

Password:

Notes:

Web Page:

Username:

Password:

Notes:

Web Page:

Username:

Password:

Notes:

Web Page:

Username:

Password:

Notes:

W

Web Page:

Username:

Password:

Notes:

Web Page:

Username:

Password:

Notes:

Web Page:

Username:

Password:

Notes:

Web Page:

Username:

Password:

Notes:

Web Page:

Username:

Password:

Notes:

Web Page:

Username:

Password:

Notes:

W

Web Page:

Username:

Password:

Notes:

Web Page:

Username:

Password:

Notes:

Web Page:

Username:

Password:

Notes:

Web Page:

Username:

Password:

Notes:

W

Web Page:

Username:

Password:

Notes:

Web Page:

Username:

Password:

Notes:

Web Page:

Username:

Password:

Notes:

Web Page:

Username:

Password:

Notes:

Web Page:

Username:

Password:

Notes:

Web Page:

Username:

Password:

Notes:

W

Web Page: _____

Username: _____

Password: _____

Notes: _____

_____

Web Page: _____

Username: _____

Password: _____

Notes: _____

_____

Web Page: _____

Username: _____

Password: _____

Notes: _____

_____

Web Page: _____

Username: _____

Password: _____

Notes: _____

_____

X

Web Page: _____

Username: _____

Password: _____

Notes: _____

_____

Web Page:

Username:

Password:

Notes:

Web Page:

Username:

Password:

Notes:

Web Page:

Username:

Password:

Notes:

Web Page:

Username:

Password:

Notes:

Web Page:

Username:

Password:

X

Notes:

Web Page:

Username:

Password:

Notes:

Web Page:

Username:

Password:

Notes:

Web Page:

Username:

Password:

Notes:

Web Page:

Username:

Password:

Notes:

X

Web Page:

Username:

Password:

Notes:

Web Page:

Username:

Password:

Notes:

Web Page:

Username:

Password:

Notes:

Web Page:

Username:

Password:

Notes:

Web Page:

Username:

Password:

Notes:

Web Page:

Username:

Password:

Notes:

X

Web Page:

Username:

Password:

Notes:

Web Page:

Username:

Password:

Notes:

Web Page:

Username:

Password:

Notes:

Web Page:

Username:

Password:

Notes:

Web Page:

Username:

Password:

Y   Notes:

Web Page:

Username:

Password:

Notes:

Web Page:

Username:

Password:

Notes:

Web Page:

Username:

Password:

Notes:

Web Page:

Username:

Password:

Notes:

Web Page:

Username:

Password:

Notes:

Y

Web Page: _____

Username: _____

Password: _____

Notes: _____

_____

Web Page: _____

Username: _____

Password: _____

Notes: _____

_____

Web Page: _____

Username: _____

Password: _____

Notes: _____

_____

Web Page: _____

Username: _____

Password: _____

Notes: _____

_____

Web Page: _____

Username: _____

Password: _____

Y Notes: _____

_____

Web Page:

Username:

Password:

Notes:

Web Page:

Username:

Password:

Notes:

Web Page:

Username:

Password:

Notes:

Web Page:

Username:

Password:

Notes:

Web Page:

Username:

Password:

Notes:

Y

Web Page:

Username:

Password:

Notes:

___

Web Page:

Username:

Password:

Notes:

___

Web Page:

Username:

Password:

Notes:

___

Web Page:

Username:

Password:

Notes:

___

Web Page:

Username:

Password:

Notes:

Z

Web Page:

Username:

Password:

Notes:

Web Page:

Username:

Password:

Notes:

Web Page:

Username:

Password:

Notes:

Web Page:

Username:

Password:

Notes:

Web Page:

Username:

Password:

Notes:

Z

Web Page:

Username:

Password:

Notes:

Web Page:

Username:

Password:

Notes:

Web Page:

Username:

Password:

Notes:

Web Page:

Username:

Password:

Notes:

Web Page:

Username:

Password:

Notes:

Z

Web Page:

Username:

Password:

Notes:

Web Page:

Username:

Password:

Notes:

Web Page:

Username:

Password:

Notes:

Web Page:

Username:

Password:

Notes:

Web Page:

Username:

Password:

Notes:

Z

Credit Card Information

Card Name: _____

Card Number: _____

Expiration Date: _____

CCV Number: _____

Customer Serv #: _____

Card Name: _____

Card Number: _____

Expiration Date: _____

CCV Number: _____

Customer Serv #: _____

Card Name: _____

Card Number: _____

Expiration Date: _____

CCV Number: _____

Customer Serv #: _____

Card Name: _____

Card Number: _____

Expiration Date: _____

CCV Number: _____

Customer Serv #: _____

Card Name: _____

Card Number: _____

Expiration Date: _____

CCV Number: _____

Customer Serv #: _____

Credit Card Information

Card Name: _____
Card Number: _____
Expiration Date: _____
CCV Number: _____
Customer Serv #: _____

Card Name: _____
Card Number: _____
Expiration Date: _____
CCV Number: _____
Customer Serv #: _____

Card Name: _____
Card Number: _____
Expiration Date: _____
CCV Number: _____
Customer Serv #: _____

Card Name: _____
Card Number: _____
Expiration Date: _____
CCV Number: _____
Customer Serv #: _____

Card Name: _____
Card Number: _____
Expiration Date: _____
CCV Number: _____
Customer Serv #: _____

Credit Card Info

Home Network Configuration

DSL/Cable Modem

Configuration URL: _____

Username: _____

Password: _____

Router

Configuration URL: _____

Username: _____

Password: _____

WiFi (Private)

SSID: _____

Key: _____

_____

WiFi (Guest)

SSID: _____

Key: _____

_____

Wireless Device 1

IP Address: _____

Username: _____

Password: _____

Wireless Device 2

IP Address: _____

Username: _____

Password: _____

Home Network

Home Network Configuration

Notes

_____

_____

_____

_____

_____

_____

_____

_____

_____

_____

_____

_____

_____

_____

_____

_____

_____

_____

_____

_____

_____

_____

_____

_____

_____

_____

_____

Authorized MAC Addresses

Host Name:

IP Address:

MAC Address

Host Name:

IP Address:

MAC Address

Host Name:

IP Address:

MAC Address

Host Name:

IP Address:

MAC Address

Host Name:

IP Address:

MAC Address

Host Name:

IP Address:

MAC Address

Host Name:

IP Address:

MAC Address

Home Network

Authorized MAC Addresses

Host Name:

IP Address:

MAC Address

Host Name:

IP Address:

MAC Address

Host Name:

IP Address:

MAC Address

Host Name:

IP Address:

MAC Address

Host Name:

IP Address:

MAC Address

Host Name:

IP Address:

MAC Address

Host Name:

IP Address:

MAC Address

Home Network

License Manager

Software:

License Number:

Software:

License Number:

Software:

License Number:

Software:

License Number:

Software:

License Number:

Software:

License Number:

Software:

License Number:

Software:

License Number:

Software:

License Number:

License Manager

Software:

License Number:

Software:

License Number:

Software:

License Number:

Software:

License Number:

Software:

License Number:

Software:

License Number:

Software:

License Number:

Software:

License Number:

Software:

License Number:

License Manager

Software:

License Number:

Software:

License Number:

Software:

License Number:

Software:

License Number:

Software:

License Number:

Software:

License Number:

Software:

License Number:

Software:

License Number:

Software:

License Number:

License Manager

License Manager

Software:

License Number:

_____

Software:

License Number:

_____

Software:

License Number:

_____

Software:

License Number:

_____

Software:

License Number:

_____

Software:

License Number:

_____

Software:

License Number:

_____

Software:

License Number:

_____

Software:

License Number:

_____

Notes

Notes

Notes

Notes

Notes

Notes

Notes

Notes

Made in the USA
Lexington, KY
02 December 2018